Imagining A New Earth

Imagining a New Earth

A Manifesto for Justice, Belonging and Human Connection

By: Alexandra Nano

Resilient Steps Publishing
United States of America

Published by Resilient Steps Publishing

ISBN: 979-8-9933817-2-5
Printed in the United States of America

Dedicated to the All
for the greater good of all

Contents

Prelude:
In The Gray

Life is duality. Sun and moon. Birth and death. Freedom and restraint. For too long, we have been taught to see the world as binary; black or white, right or wrong, good or evil. But real life does not exist at the extremes. It unfolds in the in between, in the gray.

The gray is where contradictions meet; where joy and grief live side by side, where systems can hold both harm and possibility, where justice is not simple and healing is not linear. It is the space between survival and thriving, between despair and hope.

To live in the gray is not to abandon truth but to embrace complexity. It is to admit that the stories we were told about opportunity, about safety, about justice, were not whole. And only by telling the whole truth can we begin to repair.

This book begins in the gray. It is not a story of good and evil, winners and losers. It is a story of broken systems and enduring humanity. It is a story of how we move, together, from illusion toward harmony.

IN THE GRAY

NOT BLACK.
NOT WHITE.
BUT THE SPACE BETWEEN.

SUN & MOON
JOY & GRIEF
SURVIVAL & HOPE

HERE IS WHERE WE LIVE.
HERE IS WHERE WE HEAL.
HERE IS WHERE TRUTH
AWAITS.

in the gray...

Prologue

This book is an invitation: to imagine boldly, to tell the truth, and to act with love and purpose. What follows is not a set of isolated essays but a braid of lived experience, history, and data. We trace how policy becomes personal, how budget lines shape bodies, how laws alter lives, and how collective courage can reweave what has been torn.

The New Earth imagined is not mythical. It is built on the practical: fund the foundational pillars that let people thrive, housing, healthcare, education, and insist on accountability from the systems and corporations that have long drained even exploited the worlds resources, including its most precious resource, life, all without acknowledgement, accountability or repair. The New Earth is also built on the spiritual: we belong to one another and to the planet. Balance and harmony are not slogans; they are survival strategies.

I don't write these words from theory. I write them from the ruins of a career and home stripped away, from courtrooms that treated my children and me as files to be processed instead of lives to be protected. I was caught in the impossible: housing court pushing us into eviction, family court warning me I could be charged with kidnapping if I left the state with my youngest, or abandonment if I left without him. We lost our home. We lost our community. And still, the courts refused to see us as human beings in need of safety. This is where I begin, not from comfort, but from displacement, holding one child in my arms, pushing the other in a wheelchair and carrying the weight of every family silenced by systems that pretend to protect while they destroy.

Throughout this manuscript, stories meet statistics. When we say that cutting Medicaid or underfunding the Individuals with Disabilities Education Act (IDEA), pushes families toward poverty and homelessness, we back it with evidence. When we say DEI is not a checkbox but a practice of accountability and repair, we show what that looks like in policy and in daily life.

Imagine a New Earth and then help build it.

Part 1 – The Cracks in the Old World

"Our lives begin to end the day we become silent about things that matter."
— *Martin Luther King Jr.*

Every collapse begins with fractures. Before systems fall, they splinter in classrooms, in courts, in quiet living rooms where families are left to fend for themselves.

In this part, we explore the myths we've been sold, the secrets institutions bury, and the illusions that keep us compliant. Because silence is complicity and denial only furthers the damage. To imagine a New Earth, we first have to see where the old one has already cracked.

Presence as a Radical Act

In a culture that rewards performance over presence, showing up, day after day, becomes radical. Care work is treated as invisible until it fails. But a child's nervous system does not regulate on policy promises; it regulates on reliability. The New Earth begins where a child whispers, "Don't leave me," and an adult answers, "I'm here."

I was lying next to my son, rubbing his back while we watched a show. As I got up to leave, he whispered, "Mommy, don't leave me."

"I am not leaving you, I will just be in the next room," I said. "If you need me, just say the magic word and I will come running."

He smiled. "Like a racecar."

That moment sat heavy in my chest. Because yes, I do come running. Every time. I may be stretched thin. I may be stressed out. I may be threading a needle just to get through the day. But my kids know one thing for certain: if they call out for me, I will drop everything and come running, literally. Like a racecar.

They know they are loved. They know they matter. And that counts for something. More than something. It counts for everything.

But lately I have been thinking about how families like mine, single-parent households, are spoken about, especially by people in power who have probably never spent a night on the floor next to a sick child or been so run down from the daily grind they forgot their last meal. Politicians love to promote "traditional family values" like they are some kind of moral compass. They shame single family homes while propping up outdated ideals that do not reflect the complexity and challenges of real life.

They talk about the kids from single-parent homes who end up struggling but they never talk about the ones who rise. The ones who become more resilient, more aware, more present, because they have seen what it means to survive and still choose love.

They do not talk about kids who watch a tired parent show up over and over again without needing applause, credit, or backup. The kids who learn, firsthand, what unconditional love looks like.

And they definitely do not talk about the kids raised by nannies, in boarding schools, or on FaceTime with parents who never really show up, physically there but emotionally MIA. Millionaires and billionaires preaching "family values" while outsourcing their own parenting. That part never makes it into the speech.

Because here is the truth:

Being a parent is not about being in a relationship. It is not about staying together for the Instagram photo or forcing a love that has run its course. It is about choosing your child. Over and over again. Regardless of your relationship status.

People grow. And we need to make space for that growth, to change, to evolve, to walk away without shame. It is okay to grow apart. It is okay if you are better co-parents than lovers. That does not make you broken. It makes you human.

And in doing that, choosing honesty over performance, peace over pretending, you are teaching your child something powerful. You are teaching them that love can shift and still be real. That endings are not always failures. That it is okay to let go when holding on hurts. That people can change, and that change can be gentle, impactful, and transformative.

So no, I am not a perfect mom. I lose sleep. I lose my temper. I lose pieces of myself some days. But I never lose sight of my kids. They know that one word, "Mommy," and I am there. Like a racecar.

It did not start with my children. It began earlier, in ways I did not recognize at the time. My parents got divorced when I was eight. I was daddy's little girl before that, and then, somehow, I ended up a pawn in a divorce, part of a negotiation over control and money. From a young age I learned something many people never learn: money does not make me happy. Money is not what drives me. My father began to look at me like a bill, at least in my eyes. He would pick me up and take me shopping; nothing was off limits. We would go out to eat at the same one or two restaurants, and then he would drop me off. I remember feeling unwanted, not understanding why our visits felt so empty.

I spent my school years trying to make my parents proud, getting good grades, but never feeling seen, never fitting in. People told me I had "an exotic look," whatever that meant. Olive skin. Not white, not black, not Spanish. I stopped speaking Italian when my dad left. Looking back, I do not know how the adults around me missed the signs of trauma in that young girl, but they did.

I spent the summer before sophomore year in Florida and by fall I had planned to move there after graduation. The day after I graduated high school, I got on a plane and moved. My mother came a short while later because, you know, Italian moms and attachment. The very next day I began classes at the American Institute of Massage Therapy.

Florida is an entire chapter of my life and it could be its own book, but the point remains: I have always been ambitious. I was taught that if I wanted something done, I had to do it myself. Before the age of ten, I was balancing my mother's checkbook. I learned how to use a screwdriver, a hammer, change a light bulb, and put air in my tires. I was drilled to go to college, get a good job, be independent, not to rely on anyone and if I wanted a diamond ring, to buy myself a diamond ring.

When the chance came to join DOC and his crew at the Institute for Greatly Endangered and Rare Species, I was told I had to go to college first. When I told my father I was moving to Florida and planning for college, he told me he did not care. He would just keep paying child support. I was devastated. I had expected pride. I got indifference. That moment started my disdain for money and the hollow promises that came wrapped in it.

I did trade school, worked, and eventually enrolled in undergraduate classes while holding down full-time work. I had bigger plans. I wanted a J.D. from Suffolk University, and I was working towards a postgraduate degree but when my eldest son was born, everything shifted. Yearning for degrees and prestige seems trivial after watching your child fight for his life. With no oxygen to his brain for fifteen minutes, he faced the worst prognosis. He was put on high oxygen support, organ systems stressed, fed through a tube and placed on a cooling treatment for three days to reduce further brain injury. We chose life. When I finally held him after those three days it took three nurses and a respiratory therapist to get him safely into my arms. He was fragile, and we were, in our own way, lucky.

Motherhood demanded a surrender I never anticipated, reshaping my life in ways both painful and profound. I set aside my ambitions, contentment replaced desire, I made room for hope, I rearranged everything to make space for survival and care. That choice is heavy, sometimes isolating, but it is also the only one. Being present for a child is not a sacrifice in the way society frames sacrifice. It is a deliberate refusal to let public policy, paperwork, stigma or prejudice determine whether a child lives with dignity.

That assertion leaves you exposed. As a single mother with a child who has complex medical needs, I became dependent in ways I never expected. I relied on paid caregivers, on therapists, on PCAs, on family and coworkers. I paid people, fairly. I paid above the government rates; I paid more than what my company offered for childcare. Still, dependence invites power imbalances. Even when compensated, people will behave as if they are doing you a favor rather than performing a job. They will speak to you as if you owe them something beyond money because you need them. It is never a good place to be. Not for a mother and certainly not for a child.

My life before Aiden was very different. Luxury and ease can feel like armor. Every month I had spa days with rose petal baths, massages, champagne and body scrubs. I had a generous allowance, a brand new car, automatic payments that kept me afloat. Five-hundred-dollar dinners for two, just because. But all that glittered on the outside while inside I felt dead. What looked like security masked a kind of emptiness that money, and shopping sprees could not reach.

On my birthday in 2012 during the worst fight of my life, he punched me in the face and shoved me out of his car on South Beach. People came over, asked if I was okay. We went back in the car and continued fighting. I remember taking off my shirt and throwing it out the window. I was a young, high achiever who also liked to party. Drugs were just a part of that lifestyle, there were uppers to stay up and downers to sleep, how else could anyone perform at such high levels? I walked into the kitchen like a zombie, grabbed a knife, and ended up in a psychiatric hold for seventy-two hours with stitches in both wrists.

Despite not even recognizing myself in the admission photo in my hospital file, I was screaming for him in that ward, begging to call him. He came to visit the next day with gorgeous long stem roses in hand. The first thing he said was, *"I don't hit women."* I am not saying I was innocent, a drunk birthday girl who smeared a takeout salad in his face after a broken promise of dinner on South Beach is no saint. But that doesn't excuse strangulations, his fist through my car window, or the car chases that left me gasping for air. My mother and sister flew in to check on me at the hospital, their solution was to call my father, the man I barely knew, who had been alienated from me and I, used as a pawn against him. They decided I should come "home."

By then I had that jarring feeling in my gut telling me I needed to get away. If I did not leave, I would keep returning. I might get myself in deeper trouble or I might end up dead. In 2013, I finished my bachelor's degree and left Florida for Massachusetts. I have been clean and sober ever since.

I had already begun a journey towards healing, but I still maintained that relationship for a while. That life was marked by selfishness and an unappreciation for life itself. I didn't value my own breath, my own body, or the fragility of being alive. I clung to chaos as if it were connection, attachment masquerading as love. Leaving was the shift. It was the moment I chose something different not just to survive, but to live with intention. I loved him. I was too young and inexperienced to understand he had demons of his own. Love does not always save people, especially not when their pain is turned outward as harm.

Aiden, my eldest son, deepened that transformation. His birth and survival showed me that love isn't luxury or spectacle, it's presence. It's choosing, again and again, to show up. It's reverence for life in all its forms, even when it's hard, even when it hurts. From selfishness to selflessness. From emptiness to gratitude.

He taught me about love in a way nothing else could. He taught me what is sacred and why presence matters. He taught me that life is fragile and that in the blink of an eye everything can change. I stopped living for the life I had planned and started living for what was real. As a single mother with limited support, I had to let go of many desires and expectations. People tell you to take it day by day.

For many of us, that is a luxury, so instead we take it minute by minute, sometimes breath by breath. And that's okay.

This is where the political and the personal collide. Society wants the narrative that family is a tidy, moral unit. That myth allows lawmakers and spokesmen to sound virtuous while cutting programs that enable people to be present. They preach about responsibility and tradition while voting against paid leave, adequate healthcare, and community supports that would make presence possible for working families. They lecture about motherhood while refusing to fund the systems that allow a mother to show up.

When policy and rhetoric work against the people who actually do the caring, the result is disease, trauma, and collapse.

Holy Secrets, Unholy Harm

Why do we wait until everything falls apart to offer help?

We say we care about kids. We say the first five years are everything. But what are we actually doing for the parents trying to raise those kids while battling trauma, postpartum depression, borderline personality disorder, neurodivergence, or burnout so deep they can't feel their own body?

What about the mother who is sensory sensitive, raising a child who is sensory seeking? She's overstimulated, touched out and shut down, but still getting up and doing it anyway. We act like support is a gift, something to be earned with a diagnosis, a delay, or a DCS case. But prevention is the best medicine and instead, families are handed band-aids when what they need is a lifeline.

The tools exist, but they are scattered and locked behind doors labeled "crisis." Early Intervention waits for delay. PIWI sits unused where it is needed most. Respite care is buried under red tape and years-long waitlists. Postpartum support depends on luck, insurance, and the cruel six-week cutoff.

We could offer wraparound mental health care, trauma-informed childcare, peer support, and safe spaces to breathe before the damage is done. But instead, we wait. We wait for the child to fall behind. We wait for the hotline call. We wait for harm.

Children are not resilient by default. They are resilient with support. They need safety, consistency, connection and parents who are regulated enough to provide it. Supporting parents is how we protect children, prevent crisis, and rewrite futures.

Yet our institutions too often choose silence over protection. A child can cry out. A parent can beg for justice. But if an abuser whispers it in confession, the church can stay silent and legally, it does not have to say a thing. This is not about God. It is about control, power, and institutional betrayal.

In April 2023, the Arizona Supreme Court upheld this horrifying loophole. A man confessed to sexually abusing his daughters, multiple times. The Church of Jesus Christ of Latter-day Saints knew. They said nothing. The abuse continued, justified as "confession." Church law superseded the rights and safety of children. Arizona is not an outlier. It is part of a surprising majority.

And the same lawmakers who defend this silence are the ones fighting to force a child to give birth after rape. The hypocrisy is obscene. You cannot be "pro-life" and protect predators. You cannot claim to value children while shielding those who destroy their lives. If a system protects abusers in pews instead of children in pain, that system is unholy and must be undone.

Ending clergy privilege in all 50 states is the bare minimum. No exceptions. If a child is being harmed, every adult, priest, pastor, rabbi, or otherwise must be mandated to report. Protecting children is sacred. Breaking the silence is the holy work.

And yet silence is not limited to churches. We have poured enough into broken systems that devalue the very people who keep society alive. The Center for economic and policy research reports that just 0.1 percent tax on Wall Street trades could raise over $160 billion a year, enough to fund universal pre-K, expand disability services, build public housing, and still heal the planet. But instead, we choose cycles of abuse and suffering for families and abundance for corporations.

The pattern is everywhere. Doctors of infectious diseases, whose work contains pandemics, are among the lowest-paid specialists in medicine. Early childhood educators earn less than pet groomers in many states. Housing justice advocates are overburdened and underfunded. Therapists, social workers, and disability rights attorneys are expected to labor for passion, not a living wage.

These professions do not generate wealth or promise prestige. But they prevent collapse, uphold civil rights, and change the course of lives. Still, in a society that values profit over purpose, that is not enough. They are buried in red tape, reliant on grants, and crushed by barriers that ensure only a select few can stay in the field.

This is systemic gatekeeping, redlining rebranded. Today the maps are not drawn with pens but with pay scales, credentialing requirements, inaccessible legal representation, and chronic underfunding. It is a scarcity model disguised as neutrality, starving movements that don't serve capital and exhausting the people most committed to repair.

But here is the truth: the people in these roles are not here for applause. They are here because they believe in the work. That is precisely why society has gotten away with underpaying and overloading them. But that grace will not last forever.

We pour into systems hoping for an oasis: thriving children, protected communities, vibrant futures. But everything funnels through a chokehold of red tape, suffocating the very possibilities we claim to want.

If we want safe, healthy, and just communities, we must stop rewarding flash and start funding the foundation. The question is not whether we can afford to pay these workers more. The question is how long we can afford not to.

Rights without access, without enforcement, without representation, are not rights at all and without any real accountability even real rights collapse. When oversight fails, "rights" are only theoretical. Families spend months chasing services they were promised on day one. This is why funding levels matter, not as a budget footnote, but as the difference between children and families receiving essential services or not.

For me, it means I can't just be a parent. I now carry what feels like a minor in law not just any law, but the impossible intersection of education, healthcare, parental rights, and disability advocacy. These are areas where trained attorneys specialize, and yet families like mine are expected to navigate them alone. Rights without representation are not rights at all.

It looks like judges dismissing clear violations of IDEA and urging parents to "give the school another chance," while a child loses years of services they will never get back. It looks like a housing attorney pressuring you to sign documents while you are under duress, falsifying information under oath and a judge later declaring that "you knew what you were signing." It looks like knowing you had a right to emergency housing and a stay of execution but being stripped of it anyway.

It looks like early intervention programs telling parents the first five years are critical, only for child protective services and family court to remove a toddler without transition supports, sending them off at the most delicate stage of development. It looks like a mother being forced into a room with her abuser, then dismissed as "crazy" when she names the truth. It looks like the Office of Special Education Procedures, (OSEP) insisting on the importance of transition services, and then systems releasing a child with no plan, no supports, no safety net.

This is what happens when policy lacks accountability: rights shrink into fine print, judges prioritize procedure over protection, and families are left not only traumatized but blamed for the very failures of the systems meant to serve them. Without accountability, the gap between what is promised and what is delivered becomes a canyon families are forced to cross alone, at an *immense* personal cost.

Unmasking Illusions

We are taught comforting myths: merit without context, bootstraps without boots, opportunity without access. Peeling back illusions is not cynicism; it is love. Only when we face the truth can we choose differently. We are told to "tell ourselves the truth," but how can we when the truth has been buried beneath centuries of propaganda, polished into palatability, and fed back to us as identity?

Society is drunk on illusion, high on half-truths, and addicted to comfort. Cognitive dissonance isn't just personal, it is collective. It is how entire generations sleep at night. We are told to trust systems designed in secrecy, taught that freedom is obedience, and that history is fact when, in reality, history has always been a weapon sculpted by the winners. "Tell yourself the truth" sounds noble, even enlightened, but more often what it really means is stay in your box, accept the script, and don't dig too deep.

To seek the real truth is painful and lonely. It means unraveling the stories you inherited from textbooks, religion, government, and even your own family. It is like peeling an onion with bare hands and no water in sight, each layer revealing a lie you once believed, a myth you were raised on, a choice you made thinking you had one. To tell yourself the truth is to question everything you were taught to revere, everything normalized under the guise of "that's just how it is." It requires sitting with the discomfort of realizing that the world you thought was real may have been nothing more than an elaborate illusion.

Illusions do not dissolve quietly. They fight back. And the people still living inside them will often call you crazy for walking away. Still, some of us are called to seek, to crack the veil, and to speak the truth, not just to ourselves but about the world we live in. Even if it costs us everything we thought we knew. Because the real truth does not comfort. It empowers. It transforms. It liberates.

From Narrative to Numbers

Numbers help us see the pattern beneath the story. When nearly one in five children have special health care needs, we must design for reality, not exception. MACPAC, the congressional advisory body for Medicaid and CHIP, reports that one in five children and youth have special health care needs (CYSHCN). Medicaid and CHIP are lifelines.

But numbers also reveal another truth: families are carrying rights they cannot enforce. In 2023, the Department of Education reported that millions of students with disabilities receive services under IDEA, yet less than 15% of federal funding commitments are met. That gap is not an accounting error it is a civil rights failure.

Legal deserts make the problem worse. In housing court, over 90% of tenants appear without legal representation, while landlords almost always arrive with attorneys. In education disputes, parents are routinely unrepresented, navigating laws written in complex, legal jargon while schools have lawyers on retainers. Rights exist, but families have no one to defend them.

Mental health data only reinforces what families already know. The CDC reports that nearly 1 in 5 children struggle with anxiety, depression, or behavioral challenges, yet services are often delayed or denied. Physicians report burnout at levels nearing 50%, stretched by paperwork and systemic failures instead of patient care.

Dr. Paul Farmer long warned of the impossible burdens physicians face and the urgent need for health reform, both at home and around the globe. We live in an age of breathtaking possibility, armed with technology, research, and tools our ancestors could never have imagined, yet even vaccines developed nearly a century ago remain out of reach for those who need them most. What doctors lack is not knowledge, but time, and the systems that would allow them to practice the medicine they were trained to give. Imagine carrying that weight to work each day: showing up, giving everything you have, doing everything right, only to find that bureaucracy ties your hands. The people who need help remain out of reach. Each day becomes a relentless struggle, a tug of war between light and shadow. Families, teachers, doctors, students all are pulled into a cycle of scarcity and stress that no amount of "grit" or "resilience training" can fix.

Seamus Heaney once wrote, *"History says, don't hope on this side of the grave. But then, once in a lifetime, the longed-for tidal wave of justice can rise up, and hope and history rhyme."* That line lingers like a heartbeat across generations of reformers and healers. It is a reminder that even in the teeth of bureaucracy, burnout, and betrayal, the possibility of justice remains. The work of physicians, teachers, caregivers, and families is not only about surviving today's fractured systems, but about holding open the door to that tidal wave about keeping faith that light can still win the tug of war.

The truth is this: the stories we tell of eviction, denial of services, and fractured families are not outliers. They are the predictable outcomes of systems that are underfunded, unaccountable, and unwilling to prioritize the people it claims to protect. Narrative meets numbers, and both speak the same truth: families are being set up to fail. And yet, Heaney's words remind us that the rhyme between hope and history is not automatic, it is a choice. A choice to repair what is broken, to demand systems that serve people over profit, to let justice rise like the tides and wash away the walls that keep us divided.

Part II – Systems of Exploitation

"The idea that some lives matter less is the root of all that is wrong with the world." — *Paul Farmer*

Exploitation isn't an accident. It's designed. In this part, we peel back the layers of illusion and name the systems that pretend to serve while actually harming the people they claim to protect.

Is it "inefficiency" or intentional harm?Here, we follow the money to expose how power protects itself while ordinary people pay the price. When families are retraumatized,when resources are withheld until collapse, when dignity is strippedaway in the name of policy, the system itself becomes the abuser.

The Machinery of Deception

Behind every policy debate is a balance sheet. Districts rely on Medicaid reimbursements for medically necessary school-based services documented in IEPs, a practice permitted since 1988. When Medicaid is cut, schools don't just lose 'extra' funds; they lose the ability to deliver required services.

They smile for the cameras, write checks behind closed doors, and sell your rights to the highest bidder. This is not a conspiracy theory. This is how the United States government functions, and malfunctions at the intersection of Congress, corporate lobbying, and Wall Street greed. And every time they pass a bill that sounds too shiny to be true (yes, I'm looking at you, "Big Beautiful Bill"), it's usually because it is.

Lobbying isn't just legal in the United States, it is one of the most lucrative investments a corporation can make. Insurance companies, pharmaceutical giants, oil titans, and mega-corporations all maintain entire departments or hire specialized firms to wine, dine, and influence lawmakers.

This is why insulin prices stay high. This is why Medicare is under constant threat of cuts. This is why environmental protections are gutted in the middle of a climate crisis. The answer is simple: follow the money. According to OpenSecrets, corporate lobbying expenditures reached nearly four billion dollars in 2023. That isn't charity. It is pay-to-play politics.

Corporations don't just lobby for favorable policies either; they bank on them. Every bill that reaches the floor sends signals to investors. When regulations are slashed, stocks spike. Access equals advantage, and advantage always means profit.

In healthcare, this pattern is easy to see. Public services are privatized, safety nets are slashed, and companies like UnitedHealth, Cigna, and Pfizer rack up record-breaking stock prices. Meanwhile, Americans pay more and receive less.

So-called reforms, packaged as "beautiful" solutions, often turn out to be little more than sleight of hand. Public rhetoric promises choice and efficiency, but behind the curtain the shell game continues. Cuts to Medicaid are justified as budget responsibility. High-deductible private plans expand under the guise of freedom. Federal protections disappear, even as leaders insist that consumer choice has increased.

In reality, taxpayer dollars are quietly moved away from accessible public programs and delivered straight into the hands of billion-dollar corporations.

The consequences are not theoretical and the costs are not solely monetary. Environmental protections are bargained away in exchange for oil leases and campaign donations. Nutrition programs, disability services, and basic supports for survival are gutted in the name of fiscal prudence. Families lose access to care they depend on, and communities are left to pick up the pieces.

Behind every cut, every deregulation, and every executive order is the same pattern: policy traded for profit. The cost is human, and the burden falls hardest on those already living closest to the edge.

Even when political leaders attempt to create distance between themselves and their businesses, the ties remain. Properties owned by those in power continue to profit from political activity. According to OpenSecrets, more than thirty-eight million dollars flowed into luxury properties connected to political figures between 2008 and 2024. These payments came from campaign committees, party organizations, and allied entities.

This is more than bad optics. It is a direct conflict of interest, a reminder that policy is never neutral when personal profit is involved.

In recent years, our leaders signed executive orders promising to align drug prices with the lowest international rates. This was advertised as pro-consumer reforms, but Medicare negotiations were delayed, and drug companies had more time to profit. Meanwhile, the middlemen, the Pharmacy Benefit Managers (PBM) who decide which drugs are covered were cast as the villains and targeted for reform. A convenient distraction that shifted the focus and blame away from the drugmakers who celebrated.

While Americans waited for real savings, pharmaceutical giants backed by insurance companies and an army of lobbyists, cashed in on our suffering. This is the cost of corruption. Not just polluted air and higher premiums, but children going hungry, caregivers burning out, and working families left in the dust.

And when leaders talk about "reform," the target is often Medicaid. We are told that forcing Americans off Medicaid and into the private insurance market will lower costs. In reality though, it is the opposite, it increases out-of-pocket costs, limits access to care, and funnels billions of dollars in public funding into the hands of private corporations. It is marketed as "efficiency" and "choice," but it's a sleight of hand, taking from the people to enrich the wealthy.

When services are privatized, private insurance companies get more customers. That means they can charge higher premiums, while being held to fewer standards and regulations. It's basic economics, supply and demand. When the rules are loosened and price caps are removed, corporations gain even more control. Families pay more while protections shrink. And politics makes it all possible. Donations, favors, and luxury perks keep the system friendly to corporations while ordinary people foot the bill.

If we are serious about solutions, we already know what works. International reference pricing, or "most-favored-nation" pricing, can tie U.S. costs to global standards. Empowering Medicare to negotiate directly with drug companies has the potential to save billions. Full transparency in drug development costs and profit margins would expose the truth behind the price tags. Strong, independent research and regulation is the only way to protect the public from abuse.

Unfortunately, the government often lacks the manpower and resources to even oversee these massive corporations. Agencies like the FDA and the USDA are stretched thin and underfunded. In the gaps, corporations regulate themselves, setting their own standards, writing their own rules, and grading their own homework.

The gears of the machinery of deception spin in every industry, grinding down oversight, truth, and public trust to keep profit moving forward. In agriculture, Monsanto, now Bayer, built an empire on genetically modified seeds and chemicals while lobbying to weaken safety standards. In 2018, the New York Times reported on a wave of lawsuits over glyphosate (Roundup), their flagship herbicide, which juries found had been linked to cancer.

In cosmetics, major corporations like L'Oréal and Procter & Gamble sell products with minimal oversight. The FDA does not require companies to pre-approve most ingredients before they reach consumer shelves, leaving us as test subjects in a system that prioritizes sales over safety.

In energy, Exxon and Chevron spent decades funding campaigns to deny climate change, even while their own internal research confirmed the damage fossil fuels would cause. Independent investigations and academic studies have since revealed how the industry misled the public to protect profits and have known about climate change since as early as the 1970's.

Different industries, same playbook: consolidate power, weaken oversight, and sell harm as progress.

The revolving door makes it worse. Executives move from corporate boardrooms into government offices and back again, carrying insider knowledge, influence, connections, and favors with them. What should be oversight becomes collusion. What should be protection becomes profit.

Breaking up consolidated power whether in healthcare, food, or energy is not only about limiting monopolies. It is about dismantling the machinery of deception that allows corporations to profit off the suffering and exploitation of others, corporations that masquerade as both player and referee in a game rigged against the public.

This is not just about politics. It is about people. It is about the children who lose therapy when Medicaid is gutted, and the elderly who are forced to choose between rent and prescriptions. It is the parent who skips their own medication to keep food on the table, and the worker clocking two jobs while still falling behind. It is Black and Brown families denied loans and targeted by police, Indigenous peoples watching their lands drilled and their water poisoned, immigrants exploited for labor while being denied protection, LGBTQ+ youth abandoned by policies that erase their existence, and disabled people treated as burdens instead of citizens. It is women stripped of autonomy, survivors silenced in courtrooms, and veterans returned from war only to battle homelessness and addiction. And it is the planet itself, handed to our children scorched, sold, and stripped of stewardship.

When the machinery profits from our suffering, scarcity becomes the weapon.

Scarcity as a Weapon

Scarcity is not natural. It is created when resources are hoarded at the top while families are told to fight for crumbs. It is engineered through budgets and manufactured by policies and loopholes that strip resources from families while comforting billionaires and corporations. Scarcity is not proof of limits, it is proof of theft.

I wasn't taught tax law growing up. I was taught survival.

I learned how to stretch a dollar and keep the lights on, all while being told that if I went to school and got a degree, I could buy a home and live comfortably. What I didn't know was that the same system bleeding me dry was quietly bending over backwards for billionaires like Elon Musk.

When I fled domestic abuse with my children, I was met with red tape and rejection. Emergency housing assistance? "Unavailable." Childcare subsidies? "Do not qualify." Legal assistance? "Surpassed the income threshold." Emergency help was a cruel joke, an endless loop of phone calls, recycled referrals, and hollow promises. I filled out the same forms, jumped through the same hoops, made the same desperate calls, only to be shut down again and again.

But somehow, in the same America where my wheelchair bound son, toddler and I were denied basic shelter, a billionaire was able to use stock, not cash, not income, as collateral to purchase a $44 billion company. And pay zero taxes on it.

Let that sink in.

This isn't about envy. It's about inequity.

The working class, especially mothers, especially survivors, are taxed at every turn.

We're taxed when we earn.

We're taxed when we spend.

We're taxed when we save.

We're even taxed when we die.

Meanwhile, the ultra-wealthy? They don't earn wages. They own assets. And instead of selling those assets and paying taxes like the rest of us, they borrow against them tax-free. That's how Musk bought Twitter. That's how Bezos and Zuckerberg build empires. That's how the 1% stay rich without ever lifting a finger or paying their fair share.

And Congress lets them.

Survivors like me can't write off trauma. We can't claim our unpaid caregiving hours as "investments." We don't have stock portfolios to borrow against. What we have are broken systems, trauma responses, and the constant hustle to keep our families safe and seen.

Teachers can't write off the extra hours they spend grading at midnight or the money they pour into supplies for their students. Nurses can't bill for the emotional labor of holding a patient's hand through the night. Farmers can't claim credit for feeding the country while living in poverty themselves. Communities of color can't deduct the cost of generations stolen by redlining, incarceration, and discriminatory policies. People with disabilities can't "write-off" the barriers society refuses to remove.

We are told there's "not enough" for housing, healthcare, childcare, education, or protecting the planet. But the truth is, we're not broke. We're being robbed.

What could America look like if the tax code prioritized people over profit? If trauma-informed care was funded the way tax breaks are? If caregiving and parenting disabled children came with the same incentives as capital gains? If survivors were seen not as liabilities but as the frontline of resilience and resistance? The American Dream wasn't stolen, it was taxed, gatekept, and sold to the highest bidder.

And when systems fail, families pay the price. It shows up in lost wages, missed doctor visits, mounting debt, and the invisible toll of living in constant fight or flight. The impact is immediate, it is relentless, compounding, it is generational, a crisis of mind and body passed down like an unwanted inheritance.

We are in the middle of a mental health emergency. According to the CDC's 2023 Youth Risk Behavior Survey, more than 40 percent of U.S. high school students reported feeling persistently sad or hopeless. Nearly one in five had seriously considered suicide. Among younger children, ages 3 to 17, about 11 percent have been diagnosed with anxiety, 8 percent with a behavior disorder, and 4 percent with depression. All of this is happening while the systems meant to support them are buckling under overwhelming demand.

Even the professionals' families turn to are in crisis. In 2021, nearly two thirds of U.S. physicians reported at least one symptom of burnout. More recent numbers remain high, with almost half of all doctors, especially those in primary care, at risk of leaving patient care altogether if conditions do not improve.

Depression is climbing across the country. Between 2021 and 2023, about 13 percent of people age 12 and older reported experiencing clinically significant depression. Rates are highest among teenagers, and poverty makes the picture even worse. Depression is nearly three times more common among people living below the federal poverty line.

These numbers are not random. They are the result of scarcity engineered into our systems: underfunded schools, inaccessible healthcare, unaffordable housing, and a culture that treats care as optional. The crisis is not in our children or our doctors. The crisis is in the structures that keep breaking them.

This is not stress. This is systemic injury. When IDEA is underfunded and Medicaid funding is slashed, when the professionals we rely on such as interpreters, social workers, childcare centers, teachers, advocates and public attorneys are filled beyond capacity with burnout and waiting lists, families and the institutions we rely on are left structurally unprotected. The consequences ripple through health (insomnia, stress, high blood pressure, heart attack), relationships (high divorce rates, burnout, breakdowns), and hope itself becomes a scarce resource.

Equity means shifting costs back to the systems that created the harm, funneling real funding into mental health, into stable Medicaid financing, into early intervention, into resources for parents and caregivers and supports for children so that silence isn't the default and harm isn't the inevitable outcome.

When Power Turns Predatory

When the richest 1% can profit from speculative trading while children with disabilities lose essential services, we need to ask ourselves: who is this system really working for?

There's a certain silence that follows truth when it makes people uncomfortable. Like the truth that Wall Street isn't taxed. Not in the way everyday families are. Not in the way that single parents, professionals, or caregivers navigating disability and trauma are.

I was making nearly six figures. I paid $3,000 a month in rent. I had a career I built from the ground up, and then domestic abuse shattered everything. I left to protect my children and myself. I did the right thing and I lost everything.

That's how fragile "stability" really is in this country. You can follow every rule, build a good life, do everything you're supposed to, and still end up in a system that treats you like a liability the moment you need help.

And if you have a child with a disability? You'll be met with red tape, judgment, and silence. I've had to fight for Medicaid, for special education, for the right to services my son is legally entitled to. Not because we're poor. But because he has a disability. Because the safety nets we're told exist, don't.

At the same time, I watch Wall Street break records. I watch billionaires launch into space. I watch tax loopholes widen while families like mine are buried under the weight of bureaucracy and burnout.

We are not broke. We are morally bankrupt.

Families seek help and encounter hurdles: paperwork mazes, conflicting rules, retaliation, false claims, coercive control and investigations. Systems can become accidental abusers by retraumatizing those they are meant to protect.

The system became our abuser when it severed the most sacred bond I have: my role as a mother. At a family court hearing, despite informing the judge that we were already homeless, I was told my youngest son could be placed in DCS custody if I did not comply with visitation. When I spoke out, I was deemed a flight risk. Andrew, who had just turned two, was removed from my custody. As if to twist the knife, the judge remarked that I was now eligible for a public defender because in family court, you are not entitled to free legal aid if you still have custody of your children. It was a cruel irony: only when my child was taken from me did I "qualify" for the very help and protection I had *begged* for all along.

We were not even in court for visitation or a custody hearing. I had gone there to request emergency permission to relocate because eviction was imminent. I am their sole provider and caregiver, I was proactive, seeking safety and shelter for my children.

My elderly mother, just after a cancer diagnosis and without a driver's license, was appointed as a supervisor for visits. All the while my concerns about his stability and past behavior went ignored, uninvestigated. My warnings were dismissed, my credibility eroded, and my children were placed in situations I begged the court to prevent. If abuse is defined as power wielded to control, to silence, to strip dignity, then tell me, what else would you call this?

My story is not an isolated tragedy. What happened to me in that courtroom is not just about one judge or one case. It is about policies that claim to protect families but in practice tears them apart. It is about structures that withhold help until irreversible harm has been done and then call it justice, but what it really feels like is punishment for being vulnerable. This is the gap between policy and practice.

And the truth is, being vulnerable is not rare. It is universal, it is part of being human. No matter who you are, life will eventually demand resources. At some point you will need help, you will need care or an attorney, a daycare for your child or a nursing home for your parents. None of us are exempt.

Yet, we subsidize luxury and excess while slashing services for the people who need them most. We bail out industries, not humans. We reward wealth, not care. Everyone, at some point in their life, will rely on a system that is currently failing all of us.

So where is the outrage? Maybe it feels safer to stay numb. Maybe our feeds reward distraction more than discomfort. Maybe curated routines and picture-perfect lives are easier to consume than mothers naming systemic abuse and demanding reform.

But I am not here to be consumed. I am not here to be palatable. I am here to tell the truth. Because without truth, there is no repair, and without repair, there is no New Earth.

After peeling back the lies, it becomes clear: exploitation thrives when we forget our shared humanity. Every border drawn, every budget cut, every denial of care tells the same false story, that some lives are expendable. But there is another story, one that is older and truer. As Paul Farmer reminds us, *"The only real nation is humanity."*

To live by this truth is to dismantle systems of domination and build ones of care that are rooted not in profit but in belonging. Healthcare and justice are not charity; services must be easy to access without endless hoops. Funding must be stable and reliable, something families, communities, and organizations can count on. We must measure what truly matters for our well-being not just economic outputs, but health, safety, education and dignity. And we must incentivize and reward the people and systems that provide care in every aspect: parents and caregivers, yes, but also teachers, nurses, social workers, first responders, community leaders, and neighbors who show up when it matters most because when one life is devalued, all of us are diminished. The New Earth is about building systems that will sustain all of us, children, elders, workers, patients, citizens, at every stage of life.

Part III – Rewriting Belonging

"They tried to bury us. They didn'tknow we were seeds." — *Proverb*

Belonging is not charity it is a birthright. Yet too often, families are forced to prove they are worthy of help, to navigate a maze of waitlists and denials, and to carry stigma for needing support at all.

In this part, we explore what it means to fund prevention, to honor every life as equal, and to build communities where no one is disposable. Here we begin to imagine belonging as the foundation of a just society.

The Fight for Care

Care should never be something we have to fight for. It should be the foundation of society, as essential as clean water or safe shelter. Yet in America, care is rationed, politicized, and too often denied not by doctors or specialists, but by insurance company "experts" who have never met the patient. Families are left to battle for what should already belong to them: healthcare, housing, education, and basic dignity. This is not an accident of policy but a pattern of priorities, where profit is protected and people are left to fend for themselves.

The fight for care shows up in the small cruelties that make no sense outside of a profit-driven system. An uninsured person can negotiate an ambulance ride down to a few hundred dollars, while a person who works full time pays high premiums, and carries insurance receives a bill for their remaining balance, often thousands more than the discounted rate. In this upside-down logic, the person who did "everything right" ends up punished for having insurance at all.

Then there are the families caught in the trap of high premiums and high copays. You pay every month for coverage, sometimes more than a mortgage, but when you get hurt, the real costs begin. An injury will take you out of work, which means the paycheck that covers your insurance is gone, but the copays for every doctor's visit, physical therapy session, and your prescriptions keep piling up. Instead of healthcare being a lifeline, the very act of using it pushes people deeper into debt and despair.

This is the hidden truth of private insurance: it promises protection, but too often delivers financial ruin. For the working class, the safety net is full of holes, and the fight for care becomes a fight to survive both their illness and the billing department.

And here is the reality we rarely admit out loud: we will all need care one day, disability does not come only from old age. It often comes suddenly, through malpractice, workplace injury, or an accident. No one plans to need long-term care. No one expects the system they trust to employ them, to care for them, to protect them, to be the very one that fails them. This is why Medicaid is not a handout. It is healthcare infrastructure, the system's backbone, and without it, millions are left without the support they need to recover or survive.

It might be a construction worker who falls two stories after a broken safety harness. A young woman who loses mobility after a misdiagnosed infection. A grandfather who trips on the stairs, only to learn a spinal injury has left him paralyzed. A newborn with a birth injury that changes everything before life has even begun.

These are not rare stories. They are statistics. And they are warnings.

In 2022 alone, there were 2.8 million nonfatal workplace injuries reported across the United States, many resulting in permanent disability. Unintentional injuries are the fourth leading cause of death in the country. Every five minutes, someone dies from a preventable accident. As for the healthcare system? It remains one of the most dangerous sectors, with medical errors estimated to cause over 250,000 deaths each year, and nearly 800,000 people permanently disabled or killed due to diagnostic error.

We trust our jobs, our hospitals, and our daily lives to systems. But when life strikes unexpectedly or when those systems break, we expect, we need, another one to catch us.

That's why Medicaid exists.

Medicaid wasn't created as charity or a handout. It was designed to be the safety net of last resort when everything else fails. And the truth is, it will likely touch all of us one day, because whether through aging, illness, accident, or error, we will all be disabled one day. We will all rely on care. And we will all need the systems we pay into to still be there when that day comes.

Yet those systems, especially Medicaid, are constantly under threat.

Proposals to defund or restrict Medicaid aren't just policy debates; they are decisions with life-and-death consequences for the people already harmed by the systems they were told to trust. Families with medically fragile children. Veterans with amputations. Workers with traumatic brain injuries. Seniors with dementia. These aren't edge cases. They're the reality of being human.

And before anyone suggests they "just sue," let's be clear: lawsuits take years, cost thousands, and rarely cover lifetime care. In the meantime, people need equipment, therapies, home modifications, and personal care. Medicaid is often the only way those needs are met.

Instead of safety and security these individuals face relentless audits, cuts, and eligibility reviews, as if a lifelong disability might disappear with a few forms. This isn't fiscal responsibility. It is cruelty disguised as policy.

If a person is permanently disabled due to a workplace injury, a medical error, a fall, or the natural process of aging, then Medicaid should provide lifelong, comprehensive, and trauma-informed care without the constant threat of loss.

It's time to stop treating Medicaid like a burden and start funding it like the lifeline it was always meant to be. If we expect people to work, to participate, and to survive after tragedy, then we must meet them with systems built for reality, not just spreadsheets.

Because the only thing more fragile than the human body is the illusion that we're invincible. And when that illusion shatters, Medicaid must be there, not just as a policy, but as a promise.

Prevention is the Best Medicine

When we invest in early intervention, caregiver support, and community-based services, we not only shrink downstream costs, we protect children and families from unnecessary suffering. This is public health 101 and family dignity 101. Every dollar spent upstream on access, education, and support saves lives and saves far more dollars downstream on emergency care, hospitalizations, and crisis response.

But when my youngest finally returned to me after three months of forced separation, he came back with no transition support, no services, no acknowledgment of the trauma he had endured. He was only two years old in the most critical window of brain development and the state handed him back as if nothing had happened. No early intervention follow-up. No support from DCS. No childcare or early education. Just silence.

Science tells us what this means: early childhood trauma rewires the brain. It shapes attachment, emotional regulation, even the likelihood of later involvement with the criminal legal system. By denying him continuity of care and the ability to form a strong attachment bond with any relative, they weren't just negligent, they were grooming him for mental health challenges, attachment issues, difficulty with self-regulation and increased statistical chances of later involvement with the criminal legal system, not success. What kind of system knowingly plants seeds of failure in children so young?

From the first cries of birth to the last breaths of life, the U.S. claims to be one of the most developed nations in the world. Yet our outcomes tell a different story. We have one of the worst maternal mortality rates of any developed country. Our foster youth experience staggering rates of homelessness, drug use, and incarceration. Our elderly die in nursing homes plagued with neglect and abuse. These are not accidents; they are symptoms of laws and systems designed to control rather than to care.

Family court and child protective services too often function as extensions of this cycle. Children are removed from loving, struggling parents and placed into "protective" systems that are anything but protective. Foster children are funneled into lives marked by trauma, addiction, prostitution, and prison. A large percentage end up homeless, many with disabilities left unsupported. Instead of lifting families, these systems dismantle them. Instead of stewardship, they impose surveillance, investigations, stigma, and separation.

And the cycle continues: from foster care to prison. Our system relies on this pipeline, with prisons functioning as a source of free labor. Vulnerable populations are criminalized, incarcerated, and then forced to serve free labor for industries that profit while their lives are diminished.

If America truly wanted an empowered, thriving population, our systems would look very different. They would nurture families instead of dismantling them, fund supports instead of punishment and protect dignity instead of exploiting the vulnerable. None of this is radical; it is backed by science, data, and lived experience. Yet we continue to legislate disconnection, disconnection from children, from community, from elders, from the earth itself.

The question is not whether we can afford to build better systems. The question is why, in the wealthiest nation on earth, we continue to choose laws that harm rather than heal.

Equity in Action

Inclusion is not tolerance, it is belonging. Disability is a dimension of human diversity, not a deficit to erase.

Recently, Robert F. Kennedy Jr. stated that autism is "preventable." He went on to say that many individuals with autism will never work, never pay taxes, never use the toilet independently and that autism destroys families.

Let's sit with that for a moment. The U.S. Secretary of Health and Human Services, who the president announced will oversee special education, stood before the public and used sweeping generalizations to devalue the lives of an entire subset of the population. A vulnerable subset of the population. As a parent of a child with disabilities, I wasn't shocked. I'm exhausted. Because this is the reality we live in every single day.

But what Kennedy describes isn't autism. It's ableism. A worldview where a person's value is tied to productivity -how much they can make, move or produce for the ultra-wealthy.

Donald Trump and Elon Musk have both used the R-word. Kennedy's words simply echoed the same ableist undertones.

History Has Already Proven Them Wrong

Let's revisit the "non-contributors" RFK is so concerned about:

Stephen Hawking, diagnosed with ALS, lived decades beyond his prognosis to change our understanding of the universe.

Helen Keller, who was deafblind, became a global author, speaker, and activist for disability rights.

Temple Grandin, autistic and proud, transformed the livestock industry and opened new doors for neurodivergent.

John Nash, who had schizophrenia, won a Nobel Prize and changed the field of economics.

Frida Kahlo, lived with chronic pain yet she redefined artistic expression and left a legacy of cultural pride.

These people weren't broken. They were brilliant. And not because they overcame their disabilities, but because they embraced life with them.

The Problem Isn't Autism. It's Society.

Let's talk about autism itself. Autism is not a disease to be "prevented." It is a neurological condition, a variation. Autistic brains often process information differently -more literally, more intensely, more honestly. Many autistic people have excellent pattern recognition, a unique sense of humor, deep loyalty, and a strong sense of justice.

Yes, it's a spectrum. Some individuals may need extensive supports throughout their lives. Others may live independently. But here's the truth: All of them matter. Their worth is not dependent on their tax bracket, toilet use, or job title.

And here's the part that should stop all of us in our tracks:

We are only beginning to scratch the surface of brain science. We're just starting to explore the long-term effects of traumatic brain injuries, environmental toxins, stress, and intergenerational trauma on neurological development and physiology. There is so much we do not yet know, so much left to be discovered.

And yet, the administration is cutting funding to universities and organizations engaged in this groundbreaking research. Instead of investing in understanding the human brain and supporting those whose brains work differently, we are choosing ignorance.

Worse than that, we are normalizing this ignorance. Statements like RFK's amplify what we already face as parents: the daily discrimination, the broken systems, and the assumption that our children are "less than." It tells the world that disabled lives are disposable unless they can adapt to fit the mold.

The current administration has leaned hard into narratives that cast vaccines as suspect. Warnings about acetaminophen in pregnancy, revived insinuations about vaccines and autism, and an emphasis on "environmental toxins" all reflect a shift away from prevention and toward pharmaceutical fixes. Vaccines are one of humanity's greatest public health triumphs. They have ended pandemics, saved millions of lives, and allowed children to reach adulthood free from polio, measles, and smallpox. To dismiss their impact is to deny both history and the families who buried children from preventable diseases.

But in the grey, there is complexity. The body is not a machine but a living ecosystem: a web of hormones, organs, nerves, and immune responses that interact in ways we still barely understand. The blood-brain barrier is not fully developed until early childhood. Our endocrine system, our pineal gland, and the body's intrinsic capacity to heal itself are delicate. We owe ourselves honest, evidence-based research into how the combination of vaccine ingredients administered on dense schedules, impacts a developing system. Research that isn't swayed by profit or ideology but rooted in truth.

Instead of investing in public health research and community protections though, resources are being funneled toward "autism treatments" like leucovorin. This shifts disability away from a question of rights and supports into a question of pathology to be cured. That is ableism in real time: autistic people positioned as the problem, their existence framed as the tragic outcome of pharmaceutical or parental choices, rather than as human beings deserving belonging.

Ableism thrives because fear sells. Fear of vaccines, fear of autism, fear of being different, fear of the body's own mysteries. What is lost is the truth: that vaccines have been one of humanity's greatest protections all over the world and that autistic lives are not collateral damage but part of the diverse fabric of our communities.

Curiosity, caution and care are not anti-science; they are the essence of science. We can hold two truths at once: that vaccines have saved the world from devastation, and that medicine must always keep asking hard questions about safety, timing, and cumulative effects. To love our children is to both protect them from epidemics and demand better science that honors their wholeness.

What if instead of "fixing" people with disabilities, we fixed society? What if we stopped fearing difference and started planning and designing for it? What if the conversations we had about disability weren't drenched in pity, but infused with possibility?

Aiden wants to write children's books. He loves to read, has the biggest heart, and will hit you with an unexpected zinger when you least expect it. He is full of warmth and wit, and his ideas could one day inspire other children, especially those who have never seen themselves represented on a page. Why shouldn't that be possible? Why is that dream any less valid than another child's?

He may need a little more assistance than the average person, but here's a reminder for all the RFKs and Trumps out there: In the blink of an eye, your entire life can change. One accident. One fall. One stroke. And just like that, you are disabled. So be careful. Because the wheel always turns.

My son, and millions of others like him, deserve better than fear-based narratives designed to devalue and dismiss them. They deserve respect, opportunity, and the chance to thrive on their own terms.

We are not asking for charity. We are demanding equity.

Autism is not the enemy. Disability is not a flaw. Ableism is the real threat. I write this not only as a parent, but as a witness to the power and promise of disability. The world has always been changed by people who see, move, and think differently. Let's build a future that honors that, not one that fears it.

DEI is real when it accepts responsibility for harm and funds repair from accessible transit and classrooms to pay for aides and interpreters. It's how we return to balance and harmony, together with the planet.

When my children were displaced, the court placed Andrew with people I explicitly said I did not trust. My voice as his mother was ignored. This is what systemic bias looks like: a white mother, already struggling, transitioning after domestic abuse and displaced, stripped of credibility and forced to watch one child be put in an unsafe environment while the other loses all supports and immediately begins to regress. If DEI is real, it must mean more than corporate diversity statements. It must mean accountability for decisions like this, decisions that erase a mother's agency, that fracture children's attachments, that violate the civil rights of children and place them into situations that will have long term negative impacts on their physical, mental and emotional development, these decisions were avoidable, these are the very decisions that perpetuate cycles of harm. Diversity, equity, and inclusion must include families like mine. Otherwise, it is nothing more than a slogan.

But my story is only one thread in a much larger tapestry of harm. Black and Brown families have endured generations of systemic erasure through redlining, mass incarceration, and police violence. Muslim communities face surveillance, scapegoating, and policies that criminalize faith and their very identity. Indigenous peoples continue to endure displacement from their ancestral lands and the erasure of their culture. Even animals and plants are exploited, displaced, and silenced, extinct, in the name of profit.

If DEI is real, it must mean more than corporate talking points. It must mean accountability for decisions like these decisions that erase agency, fracture attachments, and violate the basic rights of children, families, communities, and the living world. These choices have long-term consequences on physical, mental, and emotional development. They were avoidable. They are the very choices that perpetuate cycles of harm.

Diversity, equity, and inclusion must be expansive. It must include families like mine, but also the families silenced by racism, religious intolerance, colonization, and ecological destruction.

And let's be clear: DEI is still very real. You can outlaw the word, you can rewrite the numbers, but you cannot erase history or the harm that has already been done. DEI isn't an illusion, it's a receipt. You can ban the word, but you can't ban the truth.

Gender and racial bias shape who is believed and who is dismissed in courtrooms, clinics, and classrooms. Belonging requires redesigning processes, so truth doesn't depend on privilege. If a woman were in charge, do you think we'd still be debating women's rights year after year? Or would the conversation finally shift to holding men accountable?

Would we be talking about mandated vasectomies for men who abandon child after child instead of forcing women to bear every burden alone? Because right now, a man can father five children, have no legal rights to any of them, pay no child support, and still walk away untouched while the mother is left to sacrifice everything.

Marital rape wasn't fully criminalized in all 50 states until 1993. And as of today, the U.S. remains the only developed country without paid maternity leave requirements. We've come far, but the laws are still written in a way that assumes mothers are the default parents, forcing us into poverty, exhaustion, and survival mode while fathers can simply opt out.

And the children? They suffer the most. In the U.S. a person can severely harm their child and that child is still expected to attend visits with their abuser... These children are at higher risk for mental health issues, dropping out of school, and incarceration.

All the while, women escaping domestic abuse often end up homeless because the system prioritizes keeping families together over keeping mothers and children safe. Unfortunately, this is when many women end up going back to their abusers. And then, sadly, many end up a statistic. So tell me, why is it always about controlling women's bodies, but never about holding men responsible?

If a woman were in charge, would we still pretend family court is neutral? Or would we finally confront the gender bias on the bench? The fact that most judges are men, and that the courtroom, still shaped by patriarchy, too often confuses compliance with credibility and dismisses a mother's protective instincts as conflict?

Would we finally name what survivors already know? That men who fight for custody often win. That motherhood is put on trial while abuse is minimized or erased. That post-separation abuse is real. That litigation abuse is real. That when a mother protects her child, she's seen as combative but when a father pushes for custody, he's seen as committed. Yes, statistics favor the father when he shows up. But let's talk about who has to fight harder just to be heard. Survivors often lose custody not because they are unfit, but because they are afraid. Because they speak out. Because they name the harm.

This isn't mother vs. father. It's truth vs. performance. Power vs. protection. And a system that still hasn't learned to tell the difference.

Women have long been silenced, not by accident, but by design. In history books and hospital wards. In whispered accusations and courtroom reports. The pattern repeats: Women hung in town squares for knowing too much. Midwives and healers called witches. Mothers and wives called mad. Women locked in asylums for postpartum depression, for disagreeing with their husbands, for wanting more than obedience. "Hysteria" was the diagnosis given when a woman dared to speak truth without trembling. Barbaric treatments followed, lobotomies, isolation, institutionalization. And still today, the language lingers. *"She's emotional. She's unstable. She's crazy."*

As if feeling deeply is a flaw. When men show rage, they're passionate. When women do, they're a problem. Courtrooms, classrooms, clinics, the systems evolved, but the script has not. Even grief and protest are spun as pathology when the face is female. And too often, women themselves have been forced to cast stones at one another to survive. Generational trauma is not just personal; it is cultural, historical, systemic.

So I ask again, if a woman rewrote the rules, would the conversation change? Would emotion be seen as intelligence? Would care be seen as leadership? Would protection begin with listening? Because our emotions are not weaknesses, they are wisdom. They are the body's compass, not something to medicate into silence. And when we look up at the glass ceiling, we see it is already cracked. The light is breaking through. Let the ceiling shatter. Let the light in. Let the conversation finally change.

When governments value their citizens, they fund the foundations of life itself, healthcare, education, childcare, and paid maternity leave. These aren't luxuries; they are investments in stronger families. When mothers have support and resources, parents can bond with their babies, children grow up with security, and communities become safer and more stable. Divorce rates fall, escapism loses its grip, and cycles of violence and poverty weaken.

Empowering women means empowering society. Safe, supported mothers raise children with stronger attachments, healthier coping skills, and deeper moral grounding. Those children grow into adults who carry stability forward, creating happier families and safer communities. A government that invests in women doesn't just protect half its people, it builds the conditions for everyone to thrive.

And isn't that the truest form of patriotism? It's reciprocal. Show the people you love and care for them, and they will return it with loyalty, strength, and devotion.

Part IV – Remembering the Trail

History is not past, it echoes. The displacement of Native peoples, the theft of land, the erasure of cultures: these wounds reverberate through our present systems. In this part, we trace how old betrayals resurface in new disguises and how the truth, no matter how deeply buried, always reveals itself.

Remembering the trail is not nostalgia, it is accountability. Only by facing what has been buried can we choose not to live it again.

Echoes of Tears

The Trail of Tears is not just a history lesson; it is a living echo. The forced removal of Cherokee, Muscogee, Seminole, Chickasaw, and Choctaw nations in the 1830s left thousands dead. Today, families face eviction, deportation, and systemic displacement driven by poverty, gentrification, and climate change.

Families torn from their homes at gunpoint, stripped of their land, their belongings, their dignity. Thousands died along the way, from starvation, disease, and exposure to the elements, and the path west became soaked with trauma and grief. Sound familiar?

They marched hundreds of miles on foot but it wasn't just a march. It wasn't just "relocation." It was erasure. Theft. Genocide.

And here's the truth: the Trail of Tears isn't over. It echoes every time families are pushed out of their homes by corrupt landlords or broken systems. It echoes every time survivors are silenced, every time mothers and children are left without protection, every time people are forced to start over because those in power decided their lives were expendable.

It echoes in the detention centers run by ICE. It echoes in every immigration raid that rips a parent from their child. It echoes in the way Mexicans and others who are Indigenous to this continent are criminalized for crossing imaginary lines carved into stolen land.

Borders aren't real. People are. And every human being deserves dignity, safety, and belonging.

So when someone tells me displacement or deportation is "just the way it is," I will remember the Trail of Tears. And I encourage you to remember that injustice is never an accident. It's a choice.

I offer respect, love, and homage to the Indigenous peoples whose tears, lives, and lands were stolen, and I will carry their story with me as a reminder that silence only protects the oppressor.

We remember. We grieve. We rise.

Myth of Opportunity

On September 16, 1893, the U.S. government opened nearly 7 million acres of Cherokee Strip land to settlers. Within hours, the land was claimed, erasing generations of indigenous stewardship. The Land Run was celebrated as opportunity, but it was legalized theft.

The Cherokee Strip Land Run, marketed as a new beginning for settlers, another promise of prosperity on land freshly stripped from Indigenous hands. It was called opportunity, but it was displacement disguised as destiny.

That same myth evolved into what we now call the American Dream. Work hard, play by the rules, and you'll secure a better life. Yet beneath the glossy surface is another truth, one exported both at home and abroad.

Just as working families here are promised prosperity only to face college debt, job scarcity, high percentage rates and systemic discrimination, poor nations are promised "development" through U.S. loans. They're told that roads, dams, and irrigation will bring them into the global economy. But the fine print requires them to use American contractors, American consultants, and American resources. The money flows out as quickly as it flows in, leaving those countries indebted, dependent, and stripped of control over their own futures.

At home, it's families mortgaging their lives for education and healthcare. Abroad, it's entire nations mortgaged for infrastructure projects they don't truly own. In both cases, the story is the same: the dream is dangled as a carrot while the system ensures the wealth flows upward and outward.

The question is no longer whether the American Dream is broken it's whether we have the courage to dream something different, something just, something that cannot be built on another's dispossession. We're not just watching the system fail we're watching it abuse. And too many are being punished for how they break under that weight.

There's something deeply heartbreaking and enraging about watching the most vulnerable among us be failed time and again while the powerful play God.

We are told to trust the system. That it's there to protect us, guide us, provide for us. But how can we trust a system that profits from our pain? That exploits our health and labor, criminalizes our trauma, and rewards those who perpetuate harm? A system where policies are drafted in the dark and massive bills are pushed through in the dead of night, hidden from the very people they claim to serve. This is not protection. It is betrayal disguised as governance.

Every day in this country, we witness unchecked corporate power especially in the healthcare and pharmaceutical industries, manipulating legislation through lobbying and campaign contributions. Meanwhile, families go bankrupt trying to pay for insulin. Children are denied life-saving therapies. Survivors are left to navigate impossible bureaucracies just to stay afloat.

And who holds the system accountable?

We blame the addict, not the trauma. We punish the shoplifter, not the poverty. We incarcerate the protester, not the corrupt politician.

When someone lashes out against the system, it's often labeled "criminal," "terroristic," "evil." But what if it's reactive abuse? A term that many survivors of interpersonal trauma understand all too well. It doesn't excuse the harm, but it explains the rage. The desperation. The moment when someone stops begging for mercy and starts fighting back against a system that has already written them off.

We live in a country where a felon has been elected President and is threatening to strip people of their citizenship and segregate those labeled "mentally unwell." Where people are being primed for segregation in the name of "wellness." Where the narrative has shifted from freedom to fear and the most vulnerable are first on the chopping block.

So what do we expect people to do?

Some turn to alcohol or drugs to escape. Others to gangs to survive. Some commit blue collar crimes out of necessity. And even the idealists who enter politics with hope often face a brutal choice: play the game or lose everything. This isn't about broken individuals. It's about a broken system. And it's time we start naming that.

I don't condone violence. But I understand what it means to be pushed to your breaking point. To scream into the void and wonder if anyone will ever hear you. To be failed again and again while the powerful play God.

Because at the end of the day, we are not just watching a system fail, we are watching it abuse.

And it's time to stop gaslighting people into thinking their reactions are the problem, when the real issue is the violence built into the very structure of our society.

Political leaders often mirror society's shadows. In recent years, rhetoric that dismisses disability, mocks women, or minimizes racism does not create prejudice, it exposes it. The truth always reveals itself, often through those in power.

I did not vote for Trump. I do not support him or his policies. But I will say this, every time he enters office, a great deal of truth is revealed not about him, but about us.

Maybe I was naïve. Maybe I was sheltered. But it wasn't until Trump's last term in office that I fully understood how deeply embedded racism, ableism, and misogyny still are in this country. It was like the moment he was sworn in, the shadows vomited up everything we were pretending we'd already healed.

Suddenly, white supremacist groups were holding torch-lit marches at universities out in the open, unapologetically. I remember watching it with my mouth open. This wasn't the 1960s. This was happening now.

Then came the murder of George Floyd, brutal, public, daylight. The kind of execution-style policing you expect from a dictatorship, not a country that boasts "liberty and justice for all." Around the same time, Ahmaud Arbery, a black man was dragged from a truck and lynched. Lynchings. In 2020. These were not isolated events; they were echoes of a deeper rot.

There was the rise of misogyny, loud and proud. Men, grown-ass men, were suddenly bold enough to demean women in public, talk about our bodies like they were property, joke about sexual assault, and call it "locker room talk." But what more can we expect when the President himself has a long track record of publicly demeaning women and boasts, "when you're a star, they let you do it. You can do anything."

And what happened next? Sexual harassment survivors were silenced again. School-age girls faced increasing taunts and inappropriate behavior from boys who had absorbed the lesson: if the president can do it, so can I. Women's testimonies in court, in boardrooms, or at school board meetings were dismissed, mocked, or interrupted often by men emboldened by a culture that placed power over accountability.

And now, here we are again.

Karoline Leavitt, our White House Press Secretary, doesn't even try to mask her contempt. She speaks down to the very people she's supposed to serve, weaponizing her position like she's auditioning for a reality TV spinoff. She's not a leader. She's a performance piece in a show where cruelty gets the highest ratings. And I'm not entertained.

And then there's the way this administration treats individuals with disabilities. The President shows disrespect to the disabled community using the R word at campaign rallies and mocking journalists with physical disabilities. Disability has become the punchline again and children are mimicked on playgrounds while teens are mocking disabled children on Tik Tok.

These aren't isolated moments, they are cultural resets. All of the painstaking work of inclusion and awareness have been undone in what seems like seconds. And now his administration and allies are working to dismantle the supports and civil rights protections that individuals with disabilities rely on to survive. The very system designed to uphold equity and dignity are being dismantled in broad daylight.

The headlines spill over with unrest. In Nepal, citizens overthrew their government and now, for the first time, a woman serves as prime minister. Here at home, the assassination of Charlie Kirk shocked the nation, lynchings have resurfaced, and leaders lean into fear as their favorite political tool. One U.S. Senator laughed, *"we're all going to die someday"* as the community voiced concerns about Medicaid cuts. When we question their war games and gather in protest, they brand us extremists and terrorists. All, the while, we watch them slash our healthcare, build our prisons and offer $50,000 sign on bonuses for ICE officers to enforce their cruelty.

What is the expectation?

At the same time, Congress flirts with dismantling the checks and balances that have upheld our democracy for centuries and a California mayor proposes solving homelessness with free fentanyl.

Talks of segregation and deportation of U.S. citizens and threats to reproductive autonomy are somehow still up for debate in 2025. And yet, large portions of the public are more interested in Katy Perry's space ambitions than in the erosion of their rights.

This is what Trump does. He reveals the rot. He doesn't invent it, he exposes it. He gives it a microphone, a stage, and a red hat. And millions cheer. I didn't vote for Trump. But I'm not here to preach about left vs. right. I'm here to say: look around. Watch what happens when cruelty is modeled at the highest level. Watch how it infects classrooms, courtrooms, hospitals, and households.

People get brave when he's in power. Not brave in the honorable sense. Brave in the bold, loud, bigoted way that gives them permission to say the quiet parts out loud. And the scariest part? "We" elected him. Again. This isn't just about one man. It is about what he mirrors back at us, the truths he exposes. We can't unsee it now. And the question that keeps me up at night is no longer, "how did this happen?" It is, "what are we going to do now that we've seen it?"

Because the abuse is not confined to politics. Elites in every sector from Congress to Hollywood flaunt their power, exploit the vulnerable, and destroy lives. And when they finally land in prison, they still sit on mountains of stolen wealth.

This is not new. What settlers once called "opportunity" was legalized theft: another chapter in the long history of dispossession, betrayal, and erasure of Native people. History repeats itself. Today, the rich and powerful still hoard land, money, and influence, while families are stripped of their homes, their rights, healthcare, pensions, dignity, and futures.

This is not governance; it is control. And it is dressed up in the robes of Christian nationalism. They preach Jesus while refusing his path. Jesus did not build prisons or starve children, he fed, healed, and overturned the tables of money changers. These leaders do not serve

God; they serve man, and worse, they serve capital. That is a fundamental difference.

History reminds us what happens when fear and obedience become the backbone of government. After World War II, the world stood at Nuremberg and declared that crimes against humanity would not be tolerated. That vow still matters today, especially when politicians bankrolled by powerful lobbyists whether the pro-Israel machine or billionaires like the Perlmutter's fund wars abroad while hollowing out the soul of their own people. When leaders scapegoat the vulnerable and weaponize faith, they edge toward the same abyss that once put humanity on trial.

But there is another current moving through the world. Nepal shows us a nation willing to rewrite its story, electing a woman as prime minister after casting off the old. France rises in the streets. Other countries push back against corruption and demand reform. These sparks remind us that the future is not yet written. We are not condemned to live as prisoners of fear. We can reclaim our destiny.

A New Earth requires a reckoning. Learning the history. Naming the harms. Funding repair. Without it, cycles repeat. With it, we honor our ancestors and protect generations yet to come.

The Invisible Thread

At the heart of every thriving society is human connection. It is the invisible thread that binds us to one another, a force more powerful than law or currency. Connection is more than presence; it is recognition, empathy, and belonging. It is the difference between surviving alone and healing together.

When systems fracture families, isolate communities, or prioritize profit over people, that thread begins to unravel. Parents are separated from children. Elders are left to die in loneliness. Communities are divided along lines of race, religion, wealth, or politics. The result is not only poverty but despair, not only inequity but disconnection.

We have become a fractured society. Families, the foundational pillars of every culture, are breaking apart. The village, once our greatest asset, has been dismantled.

Without that web of care and accountability, children are left vulnerable, parents are left unsupported, and generations are left carrying trauma instead of wisdom.

This disconnection fuels intolerance. Racism, misogyny, antisemitism, religious intolerance, and gender bias are all symptoms of forgetting that we belong to one another. When we disconnect from each other, we disconnect from spirit. We forget that every harm ripples outward, that injustice to one community inevitably poisons the whole.

To repair society, we must repair the ways we connect. This means listening with compassion, creating spaces of belonging, and ensuring that no one is treated as disposable. Connection is not a luxury or a soft ideal. It is a lifeline. It is how we remember our shared humanity.

A New Earth will not be built on dominance, competition, or isolation. It will be built on connection and collaboration. This is the foundation upon which justice, equity, and harmony can thrive. Without connection, there is no community. Without community, there is no healing.

Human connection is both the oldest truth we carry and the newest possibility we must reclaim. It is how we will endure. It is how we will rise.

If the U.S. government could once redistribute land stolen from Native people to settlers then we can absolutely redistribute the wealth of corrupt politicians, corporations, and power-hungry celebrities who built empires on exploitation.

Don't tell me it can't be done.

Don't tell me the system can't bend.

It already has.

It already did, just not for the people who truly needed it.

Every system built on stolen breath will one day choke on its own foundation. The reckoning is not a question of if, but when. Imagining is the first step. Building is the next.

Part V – Reimagining Leadership

"The master's tools will never dismantlethe master's house." —*Audre Lorde*

The New Earth cannot be built with old blueprints. Leadership must look different: collective, accountable, rooted in equity and repair. In this part, we flip the script on power, redefine what global leadership could mean, and reclaim DEI not as a slogan but as a practice of survival.

This is where vision becomes action where we stop asking for permission and start building the future we deserve.

From Domination to Stewardship

Across traditions, the same truth emerges. The Chinese speak of *"the web that has no weaver."* Tibetans tie it into the endless loops of the Buddhist knot. Celts carved it into spirals, witches bound it into protective wards. Different names, same truth: there is no true beginning, no final end. Life is a weaving without edges.

We are each a single thread, connected to all others. Every choice, every act, every silence ripples outward, shaping the whole. To live with awareness of this is to recognize a larger order, call it spirit, ecosystem, or consciousness that holds us within it. We are not wandering aimlessly. We participates in the design.

When we understand this, we begin to imagine leadership not as dominance, but as stewardship and servitude within a living pattern. Leadership becomes service to the web itself: preserving connections, mending harm, amplifying harmony. To heal ourselves is to heal the web. To guide others is to guide the whole.

What if government regulated corporations instead of people? What if tax dollars built dignity: housing, healthcare, education not corporate bailouts? Imagining a New Earth begins with flipping this script.

The old world was built on conquest and silence. The New Earth rises from truth, balance, and belonging. Where justice is sacred, memory is honored, and life is protected.

Imagine a world where government wasn't something that loomed over individuals telling them who to love, what to ingest, or how to exist but instead operated as a force that held power accountable, redistributed wealth ethically, and ensured every human being had access to a dignified life. Not through charity. Through Justice.

For most of history, governance has been about managing people: controlling their movements, regulating their behavior, taxing their income, and punishing deviation. Meanwhile, corporations, the largest and most powerful entities in the world today, have been left to self-regulate, consolidate power, and accumulate wealth at unprecedented scales.

What if we flipped the script?

What if governance existed primarily to regulate and guide corporations, not individuals? What if taxes were collected not as a burden on everyday workers, but as a civic responsibility of corporations, scaled to their profits, carbon footprints, and impact on society? What if public budgets were designed not to subsidize industries but to liberate people, guaranteeing housing, education, healthcare, clean air, and free time?

What if corporate taxes funded the very infrastructure of freedom? Universal healthcare so no one dies from preventable illness or goes bankrupt from being alive. Public transit and green cities so people can breathe and move without burning the world. Free education so potential and progress isn't held hostage by tuition. Universal basic income or public job guarantees so survival isn't tied to wage exploitation.

This isn't fantasy. It's a shift in values. It's choosing to see the economy as a tool not a god.

Corporations are granted personhood in the eyes of the law. They enjoy protections. They influence elections. They hold wealth and power on a scale rivaling entire nations. Fine. Then let them be treated like citizens with responsibilities, obligations, and consequences.

Governments would ban lobbying that doesn't support democracy, and they would break up monopolies to foster innovation and freedom, capping corporate profits beyond certain margins unless reinvested in social good. And then they would hold CEO's criminally responsible for large scale environmental or financial harm.

A government, at its best, is the expression of its collective. It exists not to manage the people, but to protect them from exploitation, inequality, and systemic harm.

A government that GOVERNS CORPORATIONS and SERVES PEOPLE would be radical only in how deeply sane it is.

Because freedom isn't just the absence of interference it's the presence of opportunity, dignity, and care.

Imagine that.

And then: DEMAND IT.

Redefining Global Leadership

Military alliances have defined global leadership for decades. But what if we redefined leadership as protecting people, not profits? A Sacred Council of Earth would center wisdom from indigenous, ecological, and spiritual traditions.

For seventy-five years, NATO has stood as the world's most powerful military alliance, a table where high-ranking officials from thirty-two nations gather to decide matters of defense, security, and war. But what if just for a moment, we imagine something radically different?

What if instead of generals and politicians, that table was filled with the highest-ranking leaders of our spiritual traditions, indigenous nations, and wisdom keepers of the Earth?

A collaboration bound not by treaties of fear, but by a living Oath of Divine Ordinance, a promise to uphold justice, harmony, and balance with the Divine, with humanity, and with Mother Earth. A gathering of priests, rabbis, monks, shamans, medicine people and elders. A council where indigenous voices are not an afterthought but a foundational seat of wisdom. We'll call it, The Sacred Council of Earth (SCE)

Where NATO defends borders, the Sacred Council would defend balance. They would provide spiritual defense by protecting sacred sites, traditions, and lifeways with the same seriousness NATO protects airspace. With the power to declare climate collapse a spiritual emergency they would be responsible for guiding humanity back into balance and relationship with earth, the divine and one another.

Ecological leaders at the forefront of healing and reconciliation after generations of exploitation, genocide and colonization. Not with bombs and tanks, but hands, hearts, and prayers deployed where suffering is greatest. A sacred cooperation, a weaving together of wisdom traditions so that no voice is erased, and all are honored.

NATO is an alliance of governments, not peoples. At its highest level, the North Atlantic Council only nation-states have a seat. In the United States, that seat belongs to federal officials in Washington, D.C. Which means that Indigenous leaders from the United States (Navajo, Cherokee, Lakota, Seminole, and hundreds more) have no seat at NATO's table.

The same is true for First Nations in Canada and indigenous communities across all NATO countries. Their wisdom, their sovereignty, their ancestral stewardship of land and sky erased and rejected from the most powerful military conversations on Earth.

This is the gap.

And it is precisely the gap the Sacred Council of Earth would fill by ensuring that the first people of every land are not just invited but centered. When the wisdom of native people is silenced, humanity loses its oldest teachers of balance, survival, and reverence for the Earth. To imagine the Sacred Council of Earth is to imagine leadership shaped not by conquest or exclusion, but by connection, reciprocity, and responsibility to generations not yet born. This is the leap: to move from systems built in fear of each other to systems built in trust and harmony with one another.

Leadership rooted in stewardship would prioritize planetary survival, cultural preservation, and equity. A New Earth requires leaders who listen more than they command. Yes, this is a dream. But remember, so was NATO once. So was the United Nations. So was the U.S. Constitution. Every structure that exists today was imagined by someone before it was built.

The Sacred Council of Earth is both a dream and a blueprint. A reminder that we can and must reimagine what leadership looks like when old systems collapse under their own weight.

NATO was born in fear, to deter war. The Sacred Council would be born in trust, to restore harmony.

NATO asks: *How do we protect ourselves from each other?*

The Sacred Council asks: *How do we protect each other, together?*

Because the greatest threat we face is not invasion, but disconnection from one another, from spirit and from the Earth that feeds us.

Picture this, an oath of divine order, spoken in many tongues, yet one spirit: I swear not to dominion, but to stewardship. I swear not to conquest, but to care. I swear to honor the sacred breath in all beings, to uphold justice as balance, to defend life in all its forms.

This is not escapism. It is a reminder that every world we live in was once someone's dream. If governments can unite for war, humanity can unite for healing. The Sacred Council of Earth may not exist today, but it could. And maybe that's the revolution our souls have been yearning for.

Part VI – Love as the Key to Divine Consciousness

"The moment we choose to love, we begin to move toward freedom, to act in ways that liberate ourselves and others." — bell hooks

Love is not abstraction. It is action. It is covenant. It is the most radical force we have for transformation. In this part, we explore universal love as the foundation for a New Earth: love as sacred contract, love expanded through parenthood into care for all children, love expressed through governance and justice, and love as the DEI we urgently need: Diverse, Empowered, Integral.

Love is the key that unlocks this vision, the current that binds us together, and the covenant that will carry us forward.

Universal Love as a Sacred Contract

They say everyone struggles with three small words. *I love you. I need help. I am sorry.* But what if these words are not only difficult to say, what if they reveal the ways we struggle with love itself?

Love is more than an emotion. It is the fabric of existence, the sacred current connecting us to one another and to something greater than ourselves. It takes many forms: self-love, love for others, romantic love, love for community, divine love. And like any force of nature, it requires balance. When one form is lacking or excessive, we lose our way, disconnected from our highest selves and from the source of all things.

When self-love is wounded, *I need help* feels impossible to admit. Without knowing our worth, we reject support, mistaking struggle for strength. In this way, the absence of self-love turns us into martyrs: endlessly giving to others, depleting ourselves, and confusing sacrifice with holiness. Martyrdom is not love, it is self-abandonment. A body that is starved cannot nourish. A heart that is depleted cannot radiate. Universal love demands that self-love be the foundation, not an afterthought.

When romantic love has been tainted by pain, *I love you* becomes a risk, tied to fear, rejection, or loss. In these wounds, love is redefined as attachment: the frantic declaration, *I cannot live without you.* But attachment is not love, it is possession. It is love distorted by ego's grasping hands, a clinging to another in order to avoid facing the void within ourselves. True romantic love requires detachment from control. It asks for presence without ownership, intimacy without erasure.

When love for others is fractured, *I am sorry* may be the hardest to say. Apology requires humility, and when love is overshadowed by ego, accountability feels like surrender. Yet apology is not weakness. It is a form of repair, a way of realigning the current of love that flows between us. Refusal to apologize builds walls, but accountability builds bridges.

Love itself must be held in harmony.

Too much love for others without self-love leads to neglect, depletion, and exhaustion. Too much self-love without love for others breeds arrogance and narcissism. Too much attachment in romance creates obsession, while too little breeds indifference. Too much giving without receiving creates martyrdom, while too much receiving without giving breeds entitlement.

These are not flaws to be ashamed of, they are thresholds to be crossed. What if these struggles are not failures, but initiations? What if, by unlocking each form of love, we are gifted with keys, each one opening the door to deeper wisdom, higher consciousness, and a direct connection to the divine?

True self-love dissolves shame and aligns us with our worth. It allows us to say *I need help* without fear. It opens us to abundance, to receiving what was always meant for us.

Love for others expands our capacity for empathy and unity. It reminds us that we are not separate, but mirrors reflecting the same sacred light. It teaches us to say *I am sorry* not as a loss of dignity, but as an act of restoration.

Romantic love, when free of attachment, teaches surrender. It reminds us that love is not about possession but about presence. It teaches us to give without clutching, to receive without consuming.

Divine love, the highest frequency, reminds us that we are never alone. Love itself is the bridge between the seen and unseen, the human and the sacred. It allows us to live in harmony with ourselves, with one another, and with the vastness of conscious creation.

The words we struggle to say are not only expressions of emotion. They are sacred thresholds. And when we dare to cross them, we do not just heal, we awaken.

So ask yourself, what are the words you find hardest to say? And what door might they be waiting to open?

Love is not merely an emotion. It is the fabric of existence, the current that connects us to one another and to the sacred. When we misunderstand love, we fracture ourselves. When we embody love, we awaken.

This chapter follows the path of love in its many forms, showing how each one holds a key to higher consciousness and to the building of a New Earth. We begin by breaking the illusion of twin flames, a myth that has turned wholeness into a search for something missing outside ourselves. From there, we turn to parental love, how the natural devotion we feel for our children can either remain limited to bloodlines or expand outward into care for all children. We then widen the circle further, asking what love looks like when it becomes the bond between governments and their citizens.

Universal love, in its fullest form, is a sacred contract. It calls us to live not in isolation but in covenant, with ourselves, with one another, and with the systems that shape our lives. At its highest expression, it is the DEI we desperately need: a society that is Diverse, Empowered, and Integral.

Love is the key that unlocks this vision, and love is the current that binds it together.

Our confusion about love shows up in many myths but the loudest is perhaps the illusion of twin flames. The myth of the twin flame has captivated seekers, lovers, and the spiritually curious for decades. It is often painted as the idea that somewhere out there exists a perfect other half, the missing piece of our soul. Yet this is built on a false premise: that we are broken, incomplete, in need of someone external to complete us.

In truth, we are born whole. The concept of a twin flame, in its earliest esoteric roots, was never about chasing another person but about balancing the dual energies within ourselves. In Taoist philosophy, yin and yang, the receptive and the active, the lunar and the solar, exist within every being. Depth psychology echoes this: Carl Jung described the anima and animus, the feminine within the masculine and the masculine within the feminine, as necessary for psychic wholeness. When we harmonize these polarities, we are not simply better partners, we are more conscious, integrated human beings capable of touching what mystics have called the divine.

This is where Divine Consciousness lives. Not in searching for "the one," but in the radical realization that universal love flows through us already. But universal love is not sentimental fluff. It is not constant sunshine, roses, or the pastel optimism sold on greeting cards. Like real healing, it is raw, messy, and often painful. To balance our inner dualities, to let go of ego's grasp and the obsession with external validation and the material world, requires collapse and breakthrough.

Universal love is not a feeling; it is an understanding. It recognizes that we are love. To say *I cannot live without you* is not love, it is attachment, dependence, and fear. Love liberates. Love empowers. Anything that cages or reduces us is not love but possession.

Even sex, the most physical of unions, proves this point. In our culture, sex is often treated as recreation, distraction, or release. *It is just sex,* I used to say, with a naïve bravado. But years of experience stripped away that illusion. The body can be given away freely, but true intimacy, the heart, the soul, the sacred connection, cannot.

When sex is driven by escape, it numbs or shames. In Taoist philosophy, sexual energy is not casual. It is essence, or *jing*, the root of vitality, the life-force we are born with. When sex is approached as recreation rather than communion, it shatters this essence. Energy is drained, leaving the body depleted, the spirit restless, and the mind chasing the next high. What should nourish instead hollows out, leaving confusion and emptiness. When sex is stripped of its sanctity, it reflects our shadow selves that Jung spoke of. It mirrors our disconnection from self and from others. But when honored as sacred, sex becomes an immense force for unification and manifestation.

Sacred sex is prayer in motion. It is the recognition that every intimate act is an exchange, a weaving of energies that can either drain or nourish. When entered with reverence, in sacred union, it connects us deeply with ourselves, with one another, and with the divine. It does not distract from purpose but roots us in it, reminding us that the life-force within us is shared with the one we touch and with the cosmos itself.

When sex is rooted in consciousness, it awakens. It is no longer just sex. It becomes alchemy. A ritual. A portal. In Tantra, sacred sexuality is described as *maithuna*, a practice where union transcends pleasure and becomes a vehicle for merging with the divine.

That is what universal love reveals. We are not chasing fragments, we are conduits. Real love does not cling, it co-creates. Real love does not ask, *what will I do without you,* it asks *what can we manifest together while we are here. How can we serve the collective, together?* And when two people united in purpose and consciousness align, that is divine love, not because they complete each other, but because together they amplify the universal force already alive within them.

Universal Love Through Parenting

Parental love is often described as the purest love we know. A mother who stays awake through the night rocking her child, a father who works himself to the bone to provide for his family, parents who sacrifice dreams, sleep, and sometimes their health for the sake of their children. This devotion is instinctual, primal, fierce. It feels like the truest example of unconditional love.

Yet even this love, if not examined, can slip into attachment and possession. Parents sometimes see their children as extensions of themselves, projecting their unmet dreams, fears, or unhealed wounds onto the next generation. *I cannot live without my children* sounds like love, but it is dependency in disguise.

To love your own children is natural. To love all children as though they are your own is divine. Imagine a world where no child went hungry, not because parents alone bore the weight, but because every adult felt responsible for the safety and joy of the young. Imagine a world where we saw in every child's laughter, every stumble, every spark of curiosity, not just "someone else's kid," but the sacred responsibility of us all.

Indigenous traditions often hold this truth: the child is not property, not possession, but part of the community. Ubuntu, a Bantu word from southern Africa, teaches, *I am because we are.* In that worldview, your child and my child are not separate. They are threads in the same fabric. To harm one is to weaken the whole.

Universal love expands the parental instinct outward. It says, *If my child deserves safety, so does yours. If my child deserves play, learning, and dignity, so does the child across the ocean or across the street.* True parental love becomes universal when it recognizes the sacredness of every child. And when we extend that love beyond our own bloodlines, we begin to build societies where no child is left behind.

Universal Love through Governance

Governments are meant to be an extension of care for the collective. In their highest form, they are not machines of control but instruments of love expressed through policy. If universal love begins with the individual heart, then government is how that love scales across millions.

Modern states rarely embody this. Too often, governments function as if tax paying citizens are burdens on their budgets. Healthcare becomes a commodity. Education becomes a privilege. Housing becomes an asset for speculation rather than a human right. This is not love, it is abandonment dressed in bureaucracy.

Universal love in governance would look very different. It would begin with the recognition that every citizen is inherently worthy of dignity, safety, and opportunity. Policies should not be measured by profit margins but by their citizens thriving.

When a government provides healthcare, it is not charity. It is love operationalized. When it ensures quality education, it is love extended into the future. When it guarantees food, shelter, and protections, it is love as justice.

Philosophers from Confucius to Rousseau have described this as a social contract. But contracts come with conditions, clauses, and loopholes. Universal love frames it as a covenant.

A covenant says: I protect you not because you are useful, but because you are mine to care for. You are part of me.

This is not utopian dreaming. History shows us Scandinavian models of social democracy where citizens trust their governments because they see care reflected in action; Indigenous councils where decisions were weighed not just for the present but for the seventh generation ahead. In both, love was not sentiment, it was structure.

Universal love as governance demands courage. It requires leaders who see power not as dominance but as stewardship. It requires citizens who hold each other accountable not through fear but through solidarity. And it requires remembering that the true legitimacy of a government rests not on force or wealth, but on how well it embodies love for its people.

Diversity, equity, and inclusion are not corporate buzzwords; they are practices of repair. True DEI means accountability for harm done, redistribution of resources, and systemic reform to strengthen the foundations of society.

For too long, DEI has been reduced to representation without repair, inclusion without accountability. In this New Earth vision, DEI means something else entirely different: Diverse, Empowered, Integral. It means governing by means of universal love.

Diverse: We acknowledge the richness of our human family. Indigenous, Black, Women, Disabled, LGBTQ+, Immigrant, every community carrying both deep wounds and deep wisdom. To say we are diverse is to admit the truth of our history: harm was done. Entire populations were displaced, enslaved, silenced, and stripped of resources. We cannot build a future if we refuse to tell this truth. Diversity begins with acknowledgment and acceptance.

Empowered: Acknowledgment alone is not enough. Communities must be resourced, not just recognized. Empowerment means shifting power, funding what was stolen, repairing what was broken. It means creating conditions where people are not just surviving in the margins but thriving in the center. To be empowered is to live with dignity, sovereignty, and safety, conditions too often denied to marginalized families.

Integral: To be integral is to be essential. Not optional. Not "included" as a courtesy. Integral means that every community, every culture, every body is part of the structure of society itself. No one is disposable. In a New Earth, justice and compassion are not programs added later; they are the framework we build from the start. Integral means we heal together, because we cannot thrive without each other.

The DEI Manifesto

DEI IS NOT A POLICY.

IT IS REPAIR.

IT IS NAMING THE WOUNDS.

IT IS RESOURCING THE SILENED.

IT IS REMEMBERING NO ONE IS DISPOSABLE.

LESS COMPETITION.

MORE COLLABORATION.

LESS DOMINATION. MORE HARMONY.

LESS ILLUSION. MORE TRUTH.

WE ADMIT WHAT WAS DONE.

WE TAKE RESPONSIBILITY.

WE HEAL TOGETHER.

DEI IS NOT A DEPARTMENT.

IT IS A WAY OF BEING HUMAN.

DIVERSE. EMPOWERED. INTEGRAL

The DEI We Need
Diverse. Empowered. Integral.

If domination created cycles of harm, collaboration is what breaks them. "Less competition, more collaboration" is more than a phrase; it is the foundation of a just society. Competition tells us there is not enough, that for one to rise another must fall. Collaboration reminds us that abundance is possible. It requires connection, and it teaches us that we rise together or not at all. It is not red versus blue, black or white, left versus right. We are all pieces of a greater whole, waiting to be brought back together.

In DEI *(diverse, empowered, integral)*, collaboration means co-creating policies with those most harmed, not for them. It means shared power and shared resources. In community, it means building networks of care where neighbors uplift one another instead of competing. In systems, it means rejecting zero-sum policies that exploit some to benefit others, choosing instead structures that nurture the whole.

DEI is not just about representation in offices. It is about belonging in schools, access in healthcare, fairness in courts, and balance with the Earth itself. Only by coexisting in harmony can humanity and the planet thrive.

Harmony is not utopia. It is a daily practice. It begins by admitting harm, taking accountability, and then healing together. It asks us to rise beyond lower-frequency patterns of domination and move toward higher frequencies of universal love, balance, gratitude and reciprocity.

Collaboration restores harmony because it gathers the fractured pieces and brings them back into alignment. It shifts us from survival of the fittest to survival of humanity. It is how we repair what competition destroyed. It is how we bring the pieces together and make the greater whole.

This is the DEI we need: one rooted in accountability, repair, and universal love. We admit what was done. We take responsibility. We learn. We heal. And we rise together, never again regressing into patterns of domination and exclusion, but moving toward higher frequencies of truth, balance, and harmony.

In this vision, DEI is no longer a department or a policy. It is a way of being human.

Love is the key.
Love is the current.
Love is the covenant that will carry us into a New Earth.

A covenant where diversity is honored as truth.
A covenant where empowerment repairs what was broken.
A covenant where every community is integral to the whole.
A covenant where children are raised in belonging.
A covenant where governments act as instruments of care, not machines of control.
A covenant where justice is not delayed but lived.

This covenant asks us to move beyond survival into collaboration, to rise above the illusion of separation, and to remember that what we do to one, we do to all.

This is not utopia. This is the work of love embodied, system by system, heart by heart. This is how we mend the fractures of the past and shape a world where humanity and the Earth can thrive together.

Diverse. Empowered. Integral.
This is the DEI we need.
This is the New Earth we are called to create.

And the work begins now.

Afterword: A Call to Action

The New Earth is not a dream. It is a demand. It asks us to show up for one another, to question systems of power, to protect the planet, and to choose compassion over indifference.

When I write of systemic discrimination, I am not writing in the abstract. I am writing from the concrete reality of being evicted, silenced, and displaced with two children after domestic abuse. I am writing from three months without my youngest son, from watching my eldest son with disabilities lose every support he had ever known, from rebuilding in a new state without time to prepare or transfer his services. My children have paid for these failures with their earliest years, years that shape a lifetime. And yet, here we are, still standing. I write not just for my own family, but for every family trapped in systems that confuses punishment for protection. Our stories are the evidence. Our survival is the resistance. And a vision for a New Earth, built on justice, repair, and belonging is the call.

This book is not the end of the story, it is a beginning. Now, the question is not if change will come, but when and how boldly?

The call is clear: The New Earth is ours to choose. Ours to build. Ours to claim. We are the turning point. We are the shift.

This is the moment. This is the movement. This is the New Earth.

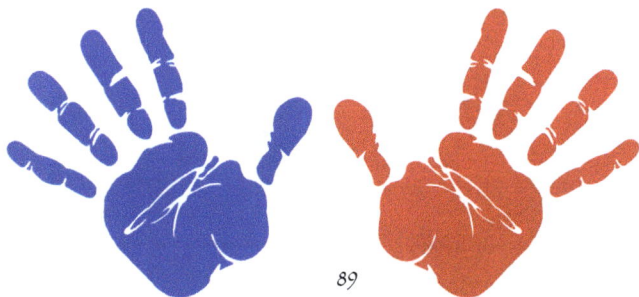

Sources & Truths:

American Medical Association. (2023). *National burnout benchmarking report.* American Medical Association. https://www.ama-assn.org/system/files/national-burnout-benchmarking-report-2023.pdf

Baker, D., Pollin, R., McArthur, T., & Sherman, M. (2009, December). *The potential revenue from financial transactions taxes.* Center for Economic and Policy Research & Political Economy Research Institute. https://cepr.net/documents/publications/ftt-revenue-2009-12.pdf

Banerjee, N., Song, L., & Hasemyer, D. (2015, September). *Exxon: The road not taken.* InsideClimate News. https://insideclimatenews.org/exxon-the-road-not-taken

BMJ Quality & Safety. (2023). *The incidence of diagnostic error in medicine.* BMJ Publishing Group. https://qualitysafety.bmj.com/content/32/9/585

Centers for Disease Control and Prevention. (2022). *Prevalence of developmental disabilities among children.* U.S. Department of Health and Human Services. https://www.cdc.gov/ncbddd/developmentaldisabilities/data.html

Centers for Disease Control and Prevention. (2023a). *Children's mental health: Data and research.* U.S. Department of Health and Human Services. https://www.cdc.gov/childrensmentalhealth/data/index.html

Centers for Disease Control and Prevention. (2023b). *Developmental disabilities monitoring network.* U.S. Department of Health and Human Services.

https://www.cdc.gov/ncbddd/developmentaldisabilities/ddmn.
html

Centers for Disease Control and Prevention. (2023c). *Unintentional injury deaths – FastStats*. U.S. Department of Health and Human Services. https://www.cdc.gov/nchs/fastats/accidental-injury.htm

Centers for Disease Control and Prevention. (2023d). *Youth risk behavior survey: Youth mental health trends*. U.S. Department of Health and Human Services. https://www.cdc.gov/healthyyouth/data/yrbs/mental-health.htm

Centers for Disease Control and Prevention. (2023e). *Depression prevalence in adolescents and adults*. U.S. Department of Health and Human Services. https://www.cdc.gov/nchs/products/databriefs/db379.htm

Centers for Disease Control and Prevention. (2023f). *Depression and poverty*. U.S. Department of Health and Human Services. https://www.cdc.gov/nchs/products/databriefs/db331.htm

Farmer, P. (2013). *To repair the world: Paul Farmer speaks to the next generation*. University of California Press. https://doi.org/10.1525/9780520954637

Georgetown University Health Policy Institute, Center for Children and Families. (2022). *Medicaid and CHIP coverage of children*. Georgetown University. https://ccf.georgetown.edu/2022/10/13/medicaid-and-chip-coverage-of-children/

Hakim, D. (2018, August 10). Monsanto ordered to pay $289 million in Roundup cancer trial. *The New York Times*. https://www.nytimes.com/2018/08/10/business/monsanto-roundup-cancer-trial.html

Johns Hopkins Medicine. (2016, May 3). *Medical errors now third leading cause of death in the U.S.* Johns Hopkins University School of Medicine. https://www.hopkinsmedicine.org/news/newsroom/news-releases/medical-errors-now-third-leading-cause-of-death-in-the-us

Kaiser Family Foundation. (2023, February 9). *Medicaid's role for children with special health care needs.* KFF. https://www.kff.org/medicaid/issue-brief/medicaids-role-for-children-with-special-health-care-needs/

Legal Services Corporation. (2022). *The justice gap: The unmet civil legal needs of low-income Americans.* LSC. https://lsc-live.app.box.com/s/xl2f3i1wv09b1zaw3l4ef4s5z1q9a9s2

Medicaid and CHIP Payment and Access Commission. (2023, March). *Children and youth with special health care needs.* MACPAC. https://www.macpac.gov/publication/children-and-youth-with-special-health-care-needs/

National Education Association. (2025). *IDEA full funding shortfall analysis.* NEA. https://www.nea.org/resource-library/idea-full-funding-shortfall-analysis

National Safety Council. (2023). *Injury facts.* National Safety Council. https://injuryfacts.nsc.org

School-Based Health Alliance. (2022). *Medicaid and school health services.* SBHA. https://www.sbh4all.org/resources/medicaid-and-school-health-services/

Social Security Administration. (2005). *The fraction of disability caused at work.* SSA. https://www.ssa.gov/policy/docs/ssb/v66n4/v66n4p31.html

Supran, G., & Oreskes, N. (2017). Assessing ExxonMobil's climate change communications (1977–2014). *Environmental Research Letters, 12*(8), 084019. https://doi.org/10.1088/1748-9326/aa815f

U.S. Bureau of Labor Statistics. (2023). *Employer-reported workplace injuries and illnesses.* U.S. Department of Labor. https://www.bls.gov/news.release/pdf/osh.pdf

U.S. Department of Education, Office of Special Education and Rehabilitative Services. (2024). *40 percent funding promise of IDEA*. U.S. Department of Education. https://sites.ed.gov/osers/2024/03/40-percent-funding-promise-of-idea/

U.S. Department of Housing and Urban Development. (2023). *Family homelessness and disability*. HUD. https://www.huduser.gov/portal/pdredge/pdr-edge-research-022023.html

U.S. Food & Drug Administration. (2022, March 16). *FDA authority over cosmetics: How cosmetics are not FDA-approved, but are FDA-regulated*. U.S. Department of Health and Human Services. https://www.fda.gov/cosmetics/cosmetics-laws-regulations/fda-authority-over-cosmetics

Acknowledgments:

This book was not written alone. I give thanks first to the Divine, whose presence has carried me through darkness and into light. To my children, who remind me daily that love is both the root and the reward of all things. To the women in my family, my mother, my grandmother, and the generations before me whose courage, sacrifices, and resilience shaped the foundation on which I stand.

I honor all women who have suffered in silence, who have endured oppression, abuse, and erasure. Your strength is a testament, and your voices, whether spoken or unspoken, are woven into these pages.

Finally, I thank myself. For choosing to rise when it would have been easier to collapse. For choosing presence over performance. For choosing love, again and again.

Sat nam.

About the Author:

Alexandra Nano is the founder of *Resilient Steps* and mother of two, including one extraordinary child with cerebral palsy. Her journey into advocacy began when she was forced to navigate broken systems in search of dignity and support, an experience that transformed her life and ignited a mission to create lasting change.

With over 20 years of experience in medicine and research, Alexandra brings both professional expertise and lived experience to her work. She has experience in direct patient care and has overseen multimillion-dollar federal research projects and collaborated with leaders at the forefront of medicine and education.

Through *Resilient Steps*, Alexandra's mission is to build a bridge between caregivers, providers and policymakers to come together and transform broken systems into structures that heal, uplift, and protect us all.

If you enjoyed this book and want to learn more about Alexandra's work, visit: www.resilientsteps.net

*9 7 9 8 9 9 3 3 8 1 7 2 5 *